# Take Care

*A Devotional for Caregivers*

DR. CHELSEA FOSTER

*Take Care With All,*

*♡ Dr. Chelsea Foster*

Spanish Version

*Cuídate: Un devocional para cuidadores*

Coming Soon

*Chloe, the mom doctor*

ISBN: 978-1-7349439-3-1

Library of Congress Cataloging-in-Publication Date is available.

Project Specialist/Publisher

Barlow Enterprises, LLC

www.destinystatement.com or text 478-227-5692

Legal Disclaimer

While none of the stories in this book are fabricated, some of the names and details may have been changed to protect the privacy of the individuals mentioned. Although the author and publisher have made every effort to ensure that the information in this book was correct at time of press, the author and publisher do not assume and hereby disclaim any liability to any party for any loss, damage, or disruption caused by errors or omissions, whether such errors or omissions result from negligence, accident, or any other cause.

Ordering Information

Books may be purchased in large quantities at a discount for educational, business, or sales promotional use. For more information or to request Dr. Chelsea Foster as the speaker at your next event, email: drchelseacares@gmail.com.

# DEDICATION

In loving memory of my mother, the late Edith Alfreda LaSmith Cutting, and my grandmother, the late Willie Alease Nibblins LaSmith. They were both women of great faith who devoted their lives in service to their families and communities. They served unselfishly and gave of all they had to make another person's day brighter.

This book is dedicated to the many caregivers I have known who give of their time and energy so that others might experience a better quality of life as a result of their faithfulness and acts of love.

I dedicate this book to my compassionate four: Charity Leigh, Chloe Marie, Charles Joshua, and Christian Wayne, as a reminder of the power, the privilege and the pure joy of being able to serve others.

I dedicate this book to my husband, Charles, who takes care of me when I forget or am unable to care for myself.

Finally, I dedicate this work back to the Lord, my God, who has graced me to persevere in all things, so that my gift of service to this world might bring Him glory. I praise you Lord, for you have been my hope and salvation since my youth. You promised to keep me when I'm old and gray, if I declare your power to the next generation. (Psalm 71 and Psalm 78).

# ACKNOWLEDGEMENTS

Thank you Lord, for the example of service that we have in Christ Jesus!

> *For even the Son of Man did not come to be served, but*
> *to serve, and to give His life a ransom for many.*
>
> — Mark 10:45

The work of a caregiver is often too big for one person. While the charge often falls on one person, successful caregiving takes the help and support of many. There are so many I would like to acknowledge, who helped me during the years when I took care of my mother while raising four children. Some helped for a season and some for a reason. Each offering of love was appreciated beyond what words could express.

First, I would like to acknowledge my immediate family. My sister, Cherelle Cutting, who worked long hours and then traveled back and forth to help take care of our mother. My sister, Cherita Jones, who was constantly praying for us and calling to check on our mom. Her voice was a source of comfort to my mother. Finally, I am grateful for my husband who could be counted on daily to help with my mother, even when it was not convenient. A person standing alone can be attacked and defeated, but two can stand back-to-back and conquer. Three are even better, for a triple-braided cord is not easily broken (Ecclesiastes 4:12). THANK YOU!

To my Uncle and Aunt, Calvin and Stephanie LaSmith: You both took on a lot to support my grandmother and mother. You were a constant support in helping my sisters and I with our mother, when she needed to be cared for. We are forever grateful for your support throughout the years. THANK YOU!

To my sister friends: Dr. Rochelle Grady, Ruth Pressley, and Alina Taylor who prayed with me, encouraged me and made themselves available to help out with the different needs that arose each week. You were my net, my sanctuary, and my rock. I am grateful to God that He put you in my life. THANK YOU!

To the spiritual communities that surrounded my family during the years I took care of my mother when my children were young, I am beyond grateful! Thank you to Vessels of Honor of Montco Bible Fellowship, to the many families of Valley Christian School, and New Life Glenside's Nursery School and Women's Ministry. Your prayers, your encouragement and your acts of love and kindness blessed me and my family through some very challenging times. THANK YOU!

# PRAISE FOR TAKE CARE

## BY EXPERIENCED CAREGIVERS

*For the last four years, I've cared for my brother and mother until they both passed, and now my father. I wish I had this devotional through those early years. Dr. Foster writes with wisdom, insight, and love! She knows the challenges and emotions that caregivers experience. Moreover, in writing this devotional, she is continuing to give care, providing love, spiritual nurture, and hope to keep us going!*

— Dr. Sharon Gramby-Sobukwe,
Associate Professor of Eastern University
Chair of the Department of Political Science Director,
Campolo Institute for Applied Research in Social Justice

Take Care *captures the emotions,* challenges, *and daily reality of caregiving. In this honest, easy to read devotional, Dr. Foster beautifully weaves together her own experiences, those of other caregivers, and scripture to encourage readers and remind them of God's grace and provision.* Take Care *invites caregivers to reflect, refresh, and refocus on their purpose.*

— Dr. Rochelle Grady, Marriage and Family Therapist

*Dr. Foster's earnest approach toward the subject of caregiving is inspirational. Reading this manuscript, encourages me to seek refuge from God, others, and stolen moments. Take Care is a wonderful escape for caregivers to be rejuvenated while reading; thereby making me aware of my own growth under such relatable topics!*

— Alina Taylor, High School Teacher

*INSPIRATIONAL! Dr. Chelsea has drawn on her personal experiences to write each devotional, which provides caregivers inspiration, encouragement and hope. The end of each devotion has a biblical passage to reflect on, and to remind the caregiver of where their "Ultimate Help" comes from.*

— Laletia Gaither, Pharmaceutical Laboratory Manager

*This book is a blessing. I believe that it will minister to the hearts of caregivers. I would recommend that every caregiver purchase this devotional and keep it close. Daily, Dr. Chelsea's words and the Word captured in these pages will bring new life with a renewed mind and heart to the reader. In these pages, she has captured my experiences as a 12-year caregiver to my father and my mother prior to their death. Dr. Chelsea has given words to my experiences that I could never have articulated. Reading her book validates my experience and comforts my soul.*

— Pamela Foster Washington, RN, MS

*The book is a great example of what a caretaker is, what a caretaker should be, and how to act as a caretaker. It takes love and the love of Jesus Christ in your heart to be a caretaker. Dr. Chelsea has given readers a lot of examples and food for thought. I feel this book will help many caregivers.*

— William Strain, Retired Public School Teacher

*The stories in this devotional are poignant and personable! As a caregiver for my older sister, who became physically and emotionally disabled after a tragic family car accident, I could identify with the caregivers in each story. Dr. Foster's is a must have for any caregiver because not too much attention is given to these "day in and day out, unsung heroes."*

— Overseer Nayjuana C. Stephens,
Life Changing Christian Fellowship, Inc.

*As a caregiver to one who is so loved, this book is a reminder of why we do what we do on a daily basis. It is a source of encouragement and a reminder that we are not alone and that GOD KNOWS. Thank you, Dr. Chelsea for taking the time to pen this book to bless others.*

— Sis. Patti Harris,
Women's Ministry Leader of Montco Bible Fellowship

*This book helped renewed my spirit! Dr. Foster's devotional for caregivers was so heartfelt and inspiring! I too find my daily strength through prayer, laughter, and self-care.*

— Quiana Bullock, PA-C, Physician Assistant

*Those who so graciously give care are, in my experience, seldom as adept at making time to take care of themselves. While the experience of sheltering in place is common in this pandemic, living with the constant stress, uncertainties, and at times the flat-out fear of feeling unable to "get out," is not new for caregivers. I had the extreme challenge and privilege of being the primary caregiver for my mother, Sondra Winters, before she transitioned in 2011. The wisdom, joy, and beauty that washes over you as you read Dr. Chelsea's stories are like feasting on your favorite comfort food on a lonely, frigid night. You cannot read this devotional without being refreshed and inspired. I did not have Take Care when I was giving care, but I am so grateful that you and I have it now!*

— Jéneen Nicole Winters-Barlow,
CEO & Co-founder, Barlow Enterprises

# CONTENTS

Foreword..................................................................................xvii

Prologue ...................................................................................1

Introduction ..............................................................................7

Day 1 Love In Action................................................................ 10

Day 2 Shut In and Closed Out.................................................. 12

Day 3 A Full Plate..................................................................... 14

Day 4 Love Never Fails.............................................................. 15

Day 5 Sandwiched In ................................................................ 17

Day 6 Not In the Plan ............................................................... 19

Day 7 Due Process..................................................................... 21

Day 8 Medication Mediation.................................................... 23

Day 9 Income Going Out .......................................................... 25

Day 10 Technically Speaking..................................................... 27

Day 11 Losing Our Way............................................................. 29

Day 12 Managing Pain Care...................................................... 31

Day 13 Be Angry........................................................................ 33

Day 14 Count It All Joy............................................................. 35

Day 15 Time to Celebrate!......................................................... 37

Day 16 No Place to Rest ............................................................ 39

Day 17 Good Medicine .............................................................. 41

Day 18 Well Kept....................................................................... 43

Day 19 Who's Keeping Watch?.................................................. 45

Day 20 Tension in the Household............................................... 47

Day 21 The Advocate ................................................................ 49

Day 22 Vegetated....................................................................... 51

Day 23 Simple Pleasures ........................................................... 53

Day 24 Above and Beyond ........................................................ 55

Day 25 The Caretaker GPS ....................................................... 57

Day 26 The Beauty of Boundaries........................................................ 59

Day 27 The Joy of the Lord.................................................................. 61

Day 28 YOU are a Great Treasure........................................................ 63

Day 29 Privileged to be a Comforter ................................................. 65

Day 30 On Your Behalf......................................................................... 67

Day 31 Blessed Assurance .................................................................... 69

Caregiver's Notes.................................................................................. 71

Author's Bio ......................................................................................... 81

# FOREWORD

Dr. Chelsea is my sister. Different mothers and fathers, but she is my sister. From our college days at West Chester University, she cared for me and many others. She was our big sister. Dr. Chelsea looked out for us struggling college students, who were a part of New Generation Campus Ministry. Not only did she pay most of our way to the various events in and out of state, but she also rented vans to transport us.

Dr. Chelsea is one of a kind. She has taken the role of the caregiver for as long as I have known her and apparently, longer.

I grew up with five brothers. I was the sole sister among my siblings. My sister passed away before I was born. I used to feel jealous that everyone in my household had a complete set, meaning, they had a daughter and a sister except me. Then I met Chelsea. At the New Generation Campus Ministry events, I experienced a breakthrough in my life, a "Coming To Jesus Moment," if you will, because I was 'something else' in college. Yet, Chelsea always made me feel accepted and loved and she hugged me and said, "You know you are my sister, right?" I cried uncontrollably because I felt that whatever I was missing in my family, I had it in her. She was a true big sister and caregiver indeed.

Allow me to substantiate Dr. Foster's spirit of caregiving.

Dr. Chelsea was a caregiver during her high school years for her aunt who lived with her briefly. Her aunt was on disability. She also cared for her grandfather who lived with her; he had Alzheimer's and was blind. I appreciated Dr. Chelsea's love and compassion years later, when I became a caregiver for my precious mother Mary, who also had Alzheimer's Disease. In her second year of undergraduate school, Dr. Chelsea drove to Philadelphia on the weekends to take food to her dad who had lung cancer and passed away before the year ended.

With her undeniably beautiful spirit, I do not recall Dr. Chelsea ever complaining. She epitomizes caregiving. Managing her growing family of six, Dr. Chelsea cared for her own precious mother through strokes, kidney failure, and hospice care. I can tell you first-hand, having experienced this with my own mother, the endurance, patience, and strength it takes to maintain your composure when the one who once held you in their arms is now in yours. She did everything from managing feeding tubes, to wound care, to doing physical and occupational therapy WHILE taking care of her own family which was, without a doubt, challenging and life changing. Caregiving requires a level of sacrificial love which Dr. Chelsea definitely has. Knowing her, she would do it all over again. That is just who she is. She epitomizes caregiving.

During this pandemic, she is currently taking care of her mother-in-love who has Dementia.

In Dr. Chelsea's remarkable book, *Take Care: A Devotional For Caregivers*, she opens up with a statement that truly resonates with those who have cared for a loved one, "A Day On, Not A Day Off!" Dr. Chelsea not only grabs our attention with this phrase that every caregiver on the planet understands, but she poignantly plants the seed of thought to consider its converse. Reading this devotional is our chance to take five minutes off so that we can be strengthened and encouraged before our day is on!

In this devotional, Dr. Chelsea bears witness with the many caregivers who have watched someone in their family serve as the caregiver. Dr. Chelsea talks about how she watched her mother and grandmother take on caregiving roles. When I was a little girl, I watched my Mom and Dad provide care for their parents and relatives.

It seems standard protocol and the norm for us caregivers. It is just what you do, in love and without complaining. Dr. Chelsea knows firsthand the characteristics, challenges, rewards, and sacrifices of caregiving, *Take Care: A Devotional for Caregivers* should be the number one book of choice for caregivers.

Dr. Chelsea designed the book to gift caregivers with a moment of self-care. The book encourages caregivers to make time for themselves, to reflect, refresh, and renew their hearts, minds, and spirits through scripture, and to be reminded that we are not alone in this caregiving journey. Dr. Chelsea adeptly infuses her own transparency by detailing her experiences in each *Day of Reflection Exercise*. These exercises serve as examples or guides that you, as the reader, can use to help you take your moment to open up and reflect. I have learned that as a caregiver, we are very used to being independent and taking care of everyone. As a result, we unknowingly forget to take care of ourselves by refusing the help that is out there. We do not want to come across as weak or needy, nor do we want to be a burden. We know what that is like and do not wish the demands of caregiving on anyone.

However, Dr. Chelsea followed her heart, knowing that there are others like herself who need a moment to themselves in order to escape daily, and for just a few minutes of whatever time we can make for ourselves to reflect, refresh and renew our heart and spirit so that we can be even better caregivers—whole and complete ones.

Are you caring for someone? Dr. Chelsea has once again taken the big sister role and paved the way in caring for the caregiver.

Take a moment to read through this devotional for the next 30 days. Stop, reflect, and renew for your own self-care. You need it. Chelsea knew that, and she answered the call to provide this outlet for you. That is what big sisters do.

*Take Care: A Devotional for Caregivers* is Dr. Chelsea's way of giving you a hug and telling you she understands and is here for you too. This is an excellent, on-time book for all caregivers who are in need of a cost-effective way to exercise self-care for the next 30 days. So go ahead, read, reflect, refresh and renew, your mind, your body, and your spirit.

This devotional will bless you real good!

Thank you, big sis!

— Dr. Sarah Renee Langley
Award-Winning Global Empowerment Speaker,
Executive Leadership Coach,
Licensed Clinical Psychotherapist, Published Author,
Loving Caregiver CEO and Founder, LeadHER International

# Prologue

I first sat down to write this in the summer of 2010 as a reflective journal. My mother had passed away in December of 2009 and my husband had just finished graduate school in May of 2010. I needed a way to process all that had transpired in the decade before. Ten years of my life had passed and I could barely remember much of it. I finished graduate school in 1998, got married in 1999, started a new job, started another new job in 2000 and gave birth in November 2001, two months after 9/11. I nursed all of 2002 and was expecting again by 2003. My second daughter came in April of 2004 and my first son in July of 2005. During this time, I had resigned from teaching high school and became an adjunct college professor, so that I could work part-time with more flexible hours. By July 2006, I gave birth to my second son, the fourth and last child. Life was challenging with four children ages four and under, but between my husband, my mother and myself, we were beginning to manage. Then life took an unexpected turn.

For over two decades, my mother had been taking care of her younger sister, who was on disability. Every Wednesday, I would go to visit her and help my mother whenever I could. In October 2006, her sister (my aunt) passed away and I was charged with taking care of the burial and other affairs. Two weeks later, a friend (unknowingly) became homeless and asked my husband and I if we could watch her daughter for a night. That night turned into almost two months. The week after she and her daughter left our home, my mom had her first mini stroke. She was in the hospital for twelve days. She recovered, but soon thereafter came to live with me and my family.

2007 felt like a sigh of relief. My mother, my husband and I were all present to take care of four children. The ratio seemed doable. We found our rhythm for getting through each day and then spring came. It started off with celebrations, like the first-year birthday of my sister's first child, followed by birthday celebrations almost every week at our home through the middle of May. It was a celebratory season that was filled with constant happiness and joy. I had accepted a new position for a summer program. In addition, my husband received an acceptance letter for a three-year graduate program in science that would begin that summer and continue every weekend throughout the school year. Everything was right in the world, until the bricks that built our life began to crumble all at the same time.

The third week of May, my mother had a major stroke, which kept her in the hospital for two months. My youngest sister and her family had just moved to Hawaii. My other sister worked very long hours and had to travel over an hour back and forth to visit. It was already challenging enough starting a new job. In addition, I no longer had my mom's support with the children and my husband was not around as much because he was in graduate school as well as working fulltime. As the primary caregiver for my four children under five years of age, I now had to arrange a schedule for round the clock care for my children so that I could work and attend to my mother at the hospital. Upon my mother's release to hospice care in July, I decided that she should stay in my home because I was told that she only had a month or two left. I knew that I would not be able to keep up the pace of working, finding childcare and visiting her in another location. It was decided! For two months, our family room would become a hospice care room, which was flooded everyday with visits from homecare workers, friends and family. Or so I thought...

The energy of being around so many loving people, the forced change of diet, along with the constant care was so healthful for my mother that she began to get stronger and gradually began to speak again, to eat without a feeding tube and to stand on her own. Each day, week, and month brought different changes and new challenges that had to be managed, while taking care of an infant, two toddlers and a preschooler at the same time. There seemed to be no end, no relief, and little to no opportunity to rest. Two to three months slowly became two to three years later. I had very little awareness of myself and how I was impacted from her first stroke in December of 2006 to the time my mother passed away in December 2009. A decade of my life had passed with many changes and unexpected twists and turns that forever changed how I saw myself in the world. More importantly, the passing of time revealed how lost and out of place I felt. I spent the next two years reconciling my mother's affairs, reconnecting with my children and immersing myself in their world, in addition to spending time again with my husband. It was then that I began to realize how many others around me needed support as caregivers so I started making myself available to encourage and support them. I remembered how I felt at midnight, waiting for my mother to go to sleep and waking up at 5:00 am to make sure that she made it through the night alright. This book was birthed out of my own cry for comfort, as well as my own pain of isolation and loneliness. It is a record of my personal experiences, combined with the caregiving experiences of those who have shared their journey with me. My hope is that each entry is relatable and offers a word of comfort, so that you might know that you are not alone.

I pray that each caregiver knows that they are important and need to take time to care for themselves. There are many who have been or will be called to the role of caring for others and it is "not for the faint of heart," as so many people have said to me. Through it all, as a caregiver, you learn that you are both stronger than you could have imagined *and* more dependent than you ever wanted to be. You are strong enough to help carry the cares of this world, yet fully dependent on whatever ounce of faith and grace you receive.

Whether you are caring for a child or an adult, know that YOU ARE NOT ALONE!

According to childtrends.org, since 2001, the percentage of children and youth with special health care needs has been steadily rising. They now comprise about twenty percent of the population. Similarly, the nation's graying population, driven by aging Baby Boomers born between 1946 and 1964, is also increasing. It currently accounts for about twenty percent of the nation's population, as reported by the U.S. Census Bureau on June 25th of this year (2020).

It is now 2020, and because of the Covid-19 pandemic, I am a caregiver once more for my mother-in-law. It has been four months since the government mandated a stay-in-place order in March. Many people are taking care of loved ones with little to no support. Regardless of the state you find yourself, whether it be a caregiver for a child, an adult, a family member or friend, know that you are not alone. There are many others who are on this journey with you. Some of you are struggling, some of you are sustaining and others of you are survivors. All of us have been impacted in some great way and our perspective on the value of life has forever been changed. Caregivers have the ability to show empathy and compassion in a way that others may not understand, unless they have been through the experience. We need to take every opportunity to embrace the role, see the privilege of being able to help another, and recognize the strength gained in the process. I salute you for your commitment to loving and holding another person in higher esteem than yourself. I love that you are God's hands on earth and an example to others of what love in action looks like.

Keep pressing on, keep loving more, be encouraged and most importantly, *Take Care*!

# Introduction

"A day on, not a day off!" It was January 16, 2012, a celebration of the life of the Rev. Dr. Martin Luther King, Jr. Coincidently, it was the day that I felt most pressed to begin this endeavor of changing my journal into an inspirational devotional for caregivers. On this day, many were gathering in Washington D.C. to observe the newly erected memorial built in his honor. Across the country, Americans joined together in a community service effort of one kind or another. People of every background, ethnicity, age and class were serving and beautifying their communities. At the end of the day, all returned home, weary and ready for a good night's rest, knowing that their participation in service to others was rewarding and with great intrinsic value, bringing joy to the heart. The grandeur of the day is best summed up in a quote by King himself, "Everyone can be great, because everyone can serve."

Ironically, most people who serve others do not always feel this sense of greatness or accomplishment. There are many who serve everyday of their lives without the support of a community, by unselfishly giving of their time, strength and resources. They are neither compensated nor rewarded for their labors. Rarely are they acknowledged for the daily sacrifices they make—hardly a "thank you" to be heard. For them, each day is just another day of being a caregiver.

It is the caregiver to whom I am directing this devotional. Caregivers give so much of themselves, both day and night. Even when they are not "on duty", their minds constantly race with thoughts of what needs to be done and how to get it all accomplished. Whether you are taking care of a child, a sibling, a spouse, a parent, relative or a friend; for caregivers, it is always "a day on." Martin Luther King, Jr. has another quote that I believe is most appropriate for caregivers. It is found in his book, *Strength to Love*:

*"The ultimate measure of a man is not where he stands*
*in moments of comfort and convenience, but where he*
*stands at times of challenge and controversy."*

There is no greater challenge than being a caregiver. What makes it a challenge? There is no easy to read, step by step manual. Each day presents its own challenge and the nights can often be the darkest and loneliest times. Caregivers are unsung heroes, who often sacrifice their hopes, dreams and most of their energy for the well-being of another. Their plight often goes unnoticed and unappreciated. The completion of a "successful day" becomes the source of joy for a restful night. I wrote this book for you.

May you know that your life has great purpose and significance. The sacrifices that you make each day have eternal rewards. Caregivers are the unseen, unsung heroes who watch after "the least of these," so that this wobbly world may continue to spin strong. Being a caregiver is not for the faint of heart, but if this charge is given to you, I implore you to consider it as a high honor of duty, service and sacrifice. It deserves no less respect than given to those who dedicate their lives to protect and serve our country.

According to the Merriam-Webster Dictionary, a "caregiver" is a person who provides direct care for individuals, such as children, elderly people, or the chronically ill. The term "caregiver" was actually coined in the 1960's. However, we all know that caregiving has been a life-long responsibility of many (particularly women), since the beginning of time. This may be you or someone you know, who is about to embark on the journey of caregiving. Regardless, I pray that this will be a resource from which many will glean and take encouragement.

With each entry, may you be reminded that you are not alone. You are not the first and most certainly will not be the last on this journey of caregiving. If you do little more than take ten minutes out of your day to read a page of this devotional and reflect, you have done yourself a great service. Take time to pray for a sincere heart, a focused mind, sustained strength and, above all, wisdom and grace as you go through your day.

*Diakoneo! Take care!*

— *Dr. Chelsea Foster*

# *Day 1*

## LOVE IN ACTION

Throughout my whole life I have watched caregivers in action. My grandmother raised six children over the span of five decades starting in the 1940's. In the 1980's, she became responsible for her grown daughter, who became disabled. At the same time, my grandfather had become blind and she had to attend to all of his needs. My mother also continued in this role as a caregiver by helping to take care of her younger brothers. She was the eldest child and ten to twenty plus years older than her siblings. Later, once my grandmother passed, my mother took over the care and responsibility for her dependent sister and her blind father who, by then, had Alzheimer's.

As caregivers, we are challenged to take care of others with love. Growing up, I saw the personal sacrifices these women made to take care of family members, while raising children and working outside of the home. My mother and grandmother served with dignity and strength; never complaining nor boasting. The example of love that they demonstrated was greatly impressed upon all who ever met them. Both women demonstrated what true love is, in the way that they cared for others. They were never rewarded nor thanked on this side of eternity. Both of them have since passed on, yet the fruit of their labors of love is still blooming in the hearts of all those they left behind.

> *If I speak with the tongues of men and of angels, but do not have love, I have become a noisy gong or a clanging cymbal. If I have the gift of prophecy, and know all mysteries and all knowledge; and if I have all faith,*

*so as to remove mountains, but do not have love, I am nothing. And if I give all my possessions to feed the poor, and if I surrender my body to be burned, but do not have love, it profits me nothing.*

*Love is patient, love is kind and is not jealous; love does not brag and is not arrogant, does not act unbecomingly; it does not seek its own, is not provoked, does not take into account a wrong suffered, does not rejoice in unrighteousness, but rejoices with the truth; bears all things, believes all things, hopes all things, endures all things.*

— 1 Corinthians 13:1-7 NASB

## Moment of Reflection

_____

_____

_____

_____

_____

_____

_____

_____

_____

_____

_____

_____

_____

_____

_____

# *Day 2*

## SHUT IN AND CLOSED OUT

It was December and my mom, who was watching my six-month-old, called me to say she was not feeling well. She couldn't focus and was afraid to stand up, so she had put the baby on the floor. My family and I were out of the area, so I immediately called both 911 and a neighbor. She had extremely high blood sugar and blood pressure. Apparently, she had been prescribed medication by her primary doctor, but had not been taking it. To make matters worse, she had not been following the diet recommended by her doctor to help bring healing. Now here she was, shut in the hospital for twelve days. This left me feeling closed out, because I was unaware of her condition and felt helpless to do anything but wait until the doctors said she was clear to go home. Could I trust her to go home by herself? What if this were to happen again? It was a few days before Christmas, so the only thing I could do to maintain peace and sanity, was to respect her wishes and let her return to her home. Later in the week, she'd join us for Christmas, so we could celebrate together. "What about the medication, mom? What are you eating? How are you taking care of yourself?" She responded, "Don't worry about me. You have your own family to take care of." However, I couldn't help it. I did worry, although there was nothing more that I could do to make the situation different, I knew I could pray to make things more bearable.

> *For this reason I say to you, do not be worried about*
> *your life, as to what you will eat or what you will drink;*

*nor for your body, as to what you will put on. Is not life more than food, and the body more than clothing? Look at the birds of the air, that they do not sow, nor reap nor gather into barns, and yet your heavenly Father feeds them. Are you not worth much more than they? And who of you by being worried can add a single hour to his life?*

— Matthew 6:25-34 NASB

## MOMENT OF REFLECTION

---

---

---

---

---

---

---

---

---

---

---

---

---

---

---

---

---

---

# *Day 3*

## A FULL PLATE

Jessie has the responsibility of taking care of her grandmother, who is on dialysis and needs insulin three times a day. Where are the other children? Where is the rest of the family? Who else can help, who's not busy or working? Who else is WILLING to make themselves available? Just ONE . . . Jessie, a full-time college student, who works hard to fulfill all of her commitments. She attends classes in the morning then spends her lunch hour at home attending to her grandmother. After lunch, she returns to school to complete her afternoon classes. She is an outstanding student and even makes time to help others. She is always cheerful and a delight to be around.

*Rejoice in the Lord always; again I will say, rejoice! Let your gentle spirit be known to all men. The Lord is near.*
— Philippians 4:4-5 NIV

## MOMENT OF REFLECTION

_____

_____

_____

_____

_____

_____

_____

# *Day 4*

## LOVE NEVER FAILS

Within a two-month period, several people close to me became care-givers. The common thread was that they each had a parent who had suffered from either a stroke or cancer AND they were raising multiple children under the age of ten! I trust that we are not given more than we can bear. However, the minute you get that first phone call or that sudden diagnosis it's as if your faith takes a free fall! "Wasn't I just complaining about trying to raise a family and keeping everything going well? I can barely keep abreast of my daily routine. I don't need another thing!" "What do you mean, doctor?" "How can this be? She or he was fine yesterday."

It's then that I remember the words of scripture and it hits me, "Man is like a flower that when the wind blows, it is gone and its place is remembered no more." Every second of time has new meaning. I begin to retrace steps that led up to this moment and try to imagine what could have been done differently. I look for an out, a way of escape and I realize that there is NO where to go but forward. So, I press on. Day by day, hour by hour, minute by minute and at the end of the week . . . I have a clearer picture of what love looks like.

> *Love will last forever! Now our knowledge is partial and incomplete, and even the gift of prophecy reveals only part of the whole picture! . . . . When I was a child, I spoke and thought and reasoned as a child. But when I grew up, I put away childish things. Now we see things imperfectly, like puzzling reflections in a mirror,*

*but soon we will see everything with perfect clarity. All
that I know now is partial and incomplete, but one day
I will know everything completely, just as God now
knows me completely. Three things will last forever—
faith, hope, and love—and the greatest of these is love.*
— 1 Corinthians 13:8-13 NLT

## MOMENT OF REFLECTION

# *Day 5*

## SANDWICHED IN

"Sandwiched In" is more than just an expression or a feeling. It really describes the way in which so many people ages 35 to 55 live today. In fact, this group is now referred to as the "sandwich generation." These are people who are caring for aging parents, while still caring for their own children. Not many are prepared and even fewer ever believed that they would even be in such a predicament.

It was springtime. The children were nine months, one, three and five years old. My husband was out of town at a conference. We spent the day with my mom watching the arborists cut down a forty-five-foot maple tree on the side of our house. Mom was so excited to share that experience with her grandchildren and decided to stay over that night. Around 5:30 in the morning, mom called my house phone from her cell phone. Her language was slurred and I could barely make out her words. I immediately ran down to the family room, where she was staying. She was having a stroke. The next two months were spent in a hospital talking with doctors about her recovery. She was to be released, yet she would still need round-the-clock care. My husband and I had much to consider. We had four small children and I had just started a part-time job. He worked full-time and had just been accepted into a graduate school program. My sister had moved out of state just two weeks earlier and my other sister frequently worked 12-hour shifts. We could only pray. Two days later, my mom was coming home with me. We did not have much time to worry or think. We could only take each day, as it came.

*Don't worry about anything; instead, pray about everything. Tell God what you need and thank him for all he has done. Then you will experience God's peace, which exceeds anything we can understand. His peace will guard your hearts and minds as you live in Christ Jesus.*

— Philippians 4:6-7 NIV

## MOMENT OF REFLECTION

_____

_____

_____

_____

_____

_____

_____

_____

_____

_____

_____

_____

_____

_____

_____

_____

# Day 6

## NOT IN THE PLAN

Dana's grandmother called. "Can you please come and clean my kitchen and make me a meal?" There are other women who live in the household. However, Dana often finds herself taking the bus to go help her grandmother, because no one else in the house will. Dana accepts the responsibility, even if it means an hour on public transportation to fulfill a one-hour task. Upon getting to the house, she opens the door and is immediately met with the 'stench of neglect.' After an hour of washing dishes and wiping down the kitchen, she bids her grandmother farewell and is back on the bus to return home. Sometimes the request is as simple as buying a bottle of soda. However, those in the house who drive will not take the time nor spend the money on anyone but themselves. Dana is a mother and a college student and has a full-time job. Why does she have to do so much for her grandmother, when there are others living in the house with her? The truth is that those who already have responsibilities are often asked to do more because they are seen as more responsible. Nonetheless, while it is not always pleasurable, the responsibility to care for another is a privilege in the sight of God.

In the Bible, Ruth understood what it meant to put the care of another ahead of her own comfort and pain. She and her mother-in-law, Naomi, had both lost their husbands. Naomi told Ruth to go her own way, so that she might find another man to marry. Naomi just wanted to be by herself; left alone to die. Ruth refused and said that she would never leave her side. A man named Boaz, heard about Ruth's faithfulness towards her mother-in-law and became in awe of her. The book of Ruth records the account of the blessing that Boaz gives to Ruth.

> *All that you have done for your mother-in-law after the death of your husband has been fully reported to me, and how you left your father and your mother and the land of your birth, and came to a people that you did not previously know. May the LORD reward your work, and your wages be full from the LORD, the God of Israel, under whose wings you have come to seek refuge.*
>
> — Ruth 2:11-12 NASB

## MOMENT OF REFLECTION

_____

_____

_____

_____

_____

_____

_____

_____

_____

_____

_____

_____

_____

_____

# Day 7

## DUE PROCESS

My mom is home now. We have been working around the clock for weeks to care for her. My sister, who is out of state, calls often to see how mom is doing. My other sister, who lives an hour away, comes several times a week to help. However, more assistance is still needed. We were referred to the elder care agency in our community to get in-house support, such as a home care doctor and a list of other services that the county can provide for us in the house. We finally got an appointment with a county social worker, who is an endless wealth of support and information. "This is great!", I thought. "When can we start?" "Well," she informs me, "just fill out this packet. I will be back in a week to pick it up and review your needs. Then, once the paperwork is submitted, I'll come back to officially open your case." "How long does all this take!?!" "About a month," she responded, "but it will be worth it, once you're in the system."

In the system? Did she not understand the urgency of this matter? Could she not hear the palpitations of my heart? Was I really going to have to wait . . . and for how long? I literally had to take this weight and lay it down. I remember praying to the Lord to calm my anxiety so that I could sleep that night. I was going to need much rest in order to even have the ability to calmly wait on the Lord.

> *O Jacob, how can you say the LORD does not see your troubles? O Israel, how can you say God ignores your rights? Have you never heard? Have you never understood?*

*The LORD is the everlasting God, the Creator of all the earth. He never grows weak or weary. No one can measure the depths of his understanding. He gives power to the weak and strength to the powerless. Even youths will become weak and tired, and young men will fall in exhaustion. But those who trust in the LORD will find new strength. They will soar high on wings like eagles. They will run and not grow weary. They will walk and not faint.*

— Isaiah 27-31 NLT

## MOMENT OF REFLECTION

_____

_____

_____

_____

_____

_____

_____

_____

_____

_____

_____

_____

_____

_____

_____

# Day 8

## MEDICATION MEDIATION

Kathy's question was, "How do I get my cousin to take her medication, so she won't get full blown AIDs? She's young with HIV and I don't want her to get any sicker."

It's hard when you love someone and you just want to do everything in your power to help them to take care of themselves. Unfortunately, sometimes their desire to be left alone outweighs your ability to force them to do what they need. In the end, they are left vulnerable and weak and you are left tired and frustrated. The battle and fatigue of taking care of another person can be so overwhelming that it can cause you to compromise your own health. Then, both of you are down. As a caregiver, you will need to fortify your mind each and every day. Emotional frustrations can turn into physical complications. It is important that you realize that it is your job to try to do what you know is right. However, the person you are caring for, will usually respond to treatments and medication according to what "feels" right to them. The only thing you as the caregiver can control, is your own peace of mind.

*Finally, brethren, whatever is true, whatever is honorable, whatever is right, whatever is pure, whatever is lovely, whatever is of good repute, if there is any excellence and if anything worthy of praise, dwell on these things. The things you have learned and received and heard and seen in me, practice these things, and the God of peace will be with you.*

— Philippians 4:8-9 NASB

# Moment of Reflection

# Day 9

## INCOME GOING OUT

He is finally out of high school, and ready to start enjoying the independent life of a college student. Unfortunately, Mike just found out that his mother has cancer. As the oldest of five children, raised by a single mother, he now has a great responsibility that he was not prepared for. Now, he is a caregiver. In between classes and working, Mike takes care of his mother. He often has to check on her throughout the day, to make sure she is alright or to see if she needs anything. Unfortunately, his mom has been in and out of the hospital. She is getting the medical attention she needs, but the bills have been mounting. The money he used to make for school goes towards paying off medical bills now. He is working more hours, getting less sleep, and feeling more stress. He believes that taking care of his mom during this time is more important than pursuing his own aspirations. His heart lies with his mother. As an adult, he could decide to do whatever he pleases with his time and money. He is free to move on and only take responsibility for himself, but he doesn't. He chooses to use his time and money to serve and help his mother.

> *It is absolutely clear that God has called you to a free life. Just make sure that you don't use this freedom as an excuse to do whatever you want to do and destroy your freedom. Rather, use your freedom to serve one another in love; that's how freedom grows. For everything we know about God's Word is summed up in a single sentence: Love others as you love yourself. That's an act of true freedom.*
> — Galatians 5:13-14 NLT

# Moment of Reflection

# Day 10

## TECHNICALLY SPEAKING

You spend your life saving for retirement; thinking of the places you'll go and the sights you'll see. Then you find yourself unable to get out of bed, waiting for someone to take you to the bathroom or to prepare your next meal. The hard-earned money you worked so long for, becomes a liability. So much money is paid out for medical expenses, prescription drugs and bulky medical equipment that within months, the thousands you had saved becomes hundreds. We were running out of resources. I called a community agency for assistance. "Technically," I was told, "your mother's assets aren't too great, so we can be of some service to you. Unfortunately, her pension is too high, so you will have to pay a copay for the services. If she were poorer, the services would be free!" Are you kidding me!?! Is this how the *system* works? If you have any assets, you are charged for social services. If you have no assets, the services are free. We were fortunate to be able to get the help we needed, but boy did we learn a lesson in bureaucracy! I was overwhelmed and realized that I could not put my trust in a system. It was then that I knew I needed to seek out additional counsel and I began to read various internet sites dealing with eldercare and finances.

*Hear my cry, O God; listen to my prayer. From the ends of the earth I call to you, I call as my heart grows faint; lead me to the rock that is higher than I. For you have been my refuge, a strong tower against the foe. I long to dwell in your tent forever and take refuge*

*in the shelter of your wings. For you have heard my*
*vows, O God; you have given me the heritage of those*
*who fear your name.*

— Psalm 61:1-4 NIV

## MOMENT OF REFLECTION

_____

_____

_____

_____

_____

_____

_____

_____

_____

_____

_____

_____

_____

_____

_____

_____

_____

_____

_____

_____

# Day 11

## LOSING OUR WAY

It was the middle of the night when I heard someone knocking things over in the kitchen below my bedroom. Everyone else in the house still seemed to be asleep. I decided to get out of bed to see what the noise was about. By the time I got downstairs, it was dark and quiet. I then saw my grandfather sitting in the chair in the corner of the room with no clothes on. He was humming and tapping his foot. "What are you doing, Pop-Pop?" I asked. He responded, "Who's that? Can you help me get out of this place? I don't know where I am and I've been trying to get out for hours!" It was then that I realized he had completely taken the wallpaper off one side of the wall near the window. I got him a blanket and walked him back to his room. He'd completely forgotten that he was planning to escape just minutes before and thanked me for helping him get back to sleep.

Anyone who had ever met my grandfather knew that he was a man of strength and dignity. As he got older, he only seemed to get stronger and more determined. The only thing that could slow him down and take him off course, however, was dementia. Towering at 6 feet 5 inches, this World War II veteran from the countryside of Scotland Neck, NC was strong enough in his seventies to walk from his home in the city where he lived, to his garden where he maintained a plot of land in the suburbs. His garden was five miles away from his home. Then, he'd walk another five miles back, after drinking just one glass of water. The mind is such a fragile thing that the slightest loss of memory or loss of reasoning can bring the tallest and strongest man to a complete halt. With each passing month,

I watched how this great man went from telling me what he wanted to do and where he wanted to go, to asking me to help him remember where and who he was. I can only imagine that this transition in life was a challenge for him. However, it also greatly affected those around him too. I watched how my mother faithfully looked after him for several years. Though sometimes frustrated, she never complained. She had put his life into God's hands and said she could only do what she could to keep him in a safe and peaceful situation. Seeing my grandfather become old and frail before my eyes made the prayer in Psalm 71:9 so real. It says, "Do not cast me off in the time of old age; do not forsake me when my strength fails." The Lord lovingly responds in Isaiah 46:4 which says, "Even to your old age and gray hairs I am he, I am he who will sustain you. I have made you and I will carry you; I will sustain you and I will rescue you."

*I am the way and the truth and the life.*

— John 14:6 KJV

## MOMENT OF REFLECTION

---

# Day 12

## MANAGING PAIN CARE

I was in and out of the hospital many times. The attendants at the valet parking knew me by sight, if not also by name. My mother was in the hospital again. The pain from the swelling in her legs had become unbearable. The sores were overwhelming. She had gotten up in the middle of the night and did not keep her legs elevated. I could not lift her legs in the morning, let alone the rest of her. Therefore, I had to call for an ambulance. My five-year-old daughter came with me to the hospital to be with her "Nonnie." We waited and waited. While doing puzzles and reading books, my little girl looked up at the posted sign and tapped me on the arm. "Look, Mommy! Nonnie will be fine. Jesus is here." "Where, I asked?" "Right there. The sign says *manger.*" Well, I started reading that sign to see the glimpse of hope that my daughter had and then I saw it. "Management . . . You have a right to pain management. The role of the hospital is to make sure that your pain is managed well. Let us know if you are experiencing pain and we will provide you with a pain manager." To my beginner reader, the "pain manager" referred to the one who was born in a manger, sent to help us manage our pain. That day I saw the hospital in a new light. It was no longer a place to go in order to receive healing. I realized that no hospital could heal anyone. Hospitals can only help people to manage the physical pain they experience. True healing comes from above. Psalm 147:3 says that the Lord heals the brokenhearted and binds up their wounds. Matthew 9:35 recounts how Jesus went about all the cities and villages, teaching in their synagogues, and preaching the gospel of the kingdom, and healing every sickness and every disease among the people. God can do more than just manage the pain of our bodies; He brings everlasting healing to our souls. Pray to receive the healing that only God can provide so that while we are in these temporal vessels, we can experience a peace that goes beyond our understanding.

> *Jesus went through all the towns and villages, teaching in their synagogues, proclaiming the good news of the kingdom and healing every disease and sickness.*
> — Matthew 9:35 NIV

## MOMENT OF REFLECTION

_____

_____

_____

_____

_____

_____

_____

_____

_____

_____

_____

_____

_____

_____

_____

# Day 13

## BE ANGRY

Am I allowed to be angry? Am I permitted to not like the circumstances I find myself in? Of course! Anger is a natural response to the feelings of frustration and disappointment that can accompany being a caregiver. Some days, it is difficult trying to take care of ourselves, let alone juggling the responsibility of maintaining the well-being of others. Where does this anger come from? How long has it been there? How long will it last? These are hard questions that only the individual experiencing the anger can answer. One thing is for sure, we must find ways to appropriately deal with anger before the anger causes us to sin and respond in ways that we might later regret. When you feel your body begin to reach a boiling point, it is best to take a "time-out." It may even be helpful to find someone to talk to or some way to release the frustration, like participating in a hobby or activity or by simply taking a nap. If the anger begins to consume your mind throughout the day, or several times a week, then it might be wise to seek help from a professional counselor or a support group. Being a caregiver is not easy. It can test the emotions. What is most beneficial is to learn how to be angry and not sin.

*Jesus went through all the towns and villages, teaching in their synagogues, proclaiming the good news of the kingdom and healing every disease and sickness.*
— Ephesians 4:26-27 NIV

# Moment of Reflection

# Day 14

## COUNT IT ALL JOY

What a request! We are each given obstacles, challenges and trials in this life. Some are more trying and painful than others. Yet, we are to count it ALL joy. How do we do that? The answer is "with patience." There is much to be learned from the book of James in the Bible. It instructs us on how to live, when we find ourselves in difficult situations. You may feel as if your faith is constantly being tested and perhaps more than others. You may even find yourself crying out, "It's not fair!" May your response be to seek God's perspective in the situation. Ask the Lord how you should respond. Ask the Lord to give you the patience and understanding to be able to endure.

> *My brethren, count it all joy when you fall into various trials, knowing that the testing of your faith produces patience. But let patience have its perfect work, that you may be perfect and complete, lacking nothing. If any of you lacks wisdom, let him ask of God, who gives to all liberally and without reproach, and it will be given to him.*
>
> *— James 1:2-5 NKJV*

# Moment of Reflection

# *Day 15*

## TIME TO CELEBRATE!

In the Bible, the book of Leviticus established many laws for the people of Israel to show them how to honor and live in relationship with a Holy God. There were even laws that commanded them to celebrate with thanksgiving unto the Lord, because He brought them through many trials and provided for them during their times of greatest need. Sometimes being a caregiver can be draining and your days feel as if you are going from morning to *mourning*, instead of mercy to mercy. Every week that passes should bring about a new opportunity to celebrate! There are days when you don't know how you are going to make it to the end. There are weeks that seem as if the end will never come... but it does! We need to thank God and give Him praise! Make a cake or a card and share it with your loved one. Be creative. Play a celebratory song, dance, sing, find a special place to go or make the place where you are special with flowers and balloons. Whatever you do, know that it's all right to take time to celebrate! The Lord has commanded it!

The summer of my mom's stroke, our family was planning to meet for a memorial service for my aunt combined with a family reunion. The week of the memorial reunion, my mother went into the hospital and was released to a rehabilitation center. Planning a memorial service and an extended reunion weekend with four small children while trying to be present for my mother was enough to make me want to shut it all down. However, I thought about the blessing of her having so much of her family in town. She would not want the get together to be cancelled on account of her. So, over that

37

weekend, along with the support of the rehab staff, we arranged for all the guests to visit with my mother throughout the weekend. She was overjoyed to see so many familiar faces. She laughed and cried all weekend long. What a celebration it was!

> *On the fifteenth day...you shall celebrate! I am the Lord your God!*
>
> — Leviticus 23:39, 43 ESV

## MOMENT OF REFLECTION

_____

_____

_____

_____

_____

_____

_____

_____

_____

_____

_____

_____

_____

_____

_____

_____

_____

_____

# Day 16

## NO PLACE TO REST

The dove is one of my favorite symbols for a myriad of reasons. It is a symbol of peace, freedom, love and in the Christian tradition – the Holy Spirit of God. It is such an innocent creature that is gifted with the ability to always find its way home. Because of its gift, the dove has been given the task of being "the messenger bird." Throughout the centuries, doves have been given the great responsibility to deliver important messages that could determine whether a great many people would either live or die. What person would knowingly and willingly agree to take on such a job? I certainly know that I would not want the fate of someone's life in my hands. However, fortunately, God knows best. He knew that the dove would and could be the faithful creature that He created it to be. Therefore, Noah sent forth a dove to search for land as proof that he, his family and all the creatures of the earth were safe, because the flood was over.

I could only imagine being that dove having to fly around for seven days, without a place to land. How tired that poor bird must have been! How hopeless and frustrated it must have felt flying around by itself without the company of other birds. The poor dove had nowhere to rest its feet! To the other animals on the ark, it might have looked as if the bird was abandoned and sent to take care of itself. Why not choose some other creature from the ark? Why would God give this little bird such a great responsibility? He did so because He is a great God with a great plan. He knew that the little dove was exactly what Noah needed to provide assurance that his family would make it through the flood. The dove flew around for seven days. I can only imagine that each day felt longer than the previous one. However, between each flight, Noah called the dove back so that it could rest. If God took care of the dove, how much more does He value and care for us, His children, when we are left to carry out a great responsibility?

*But the dove found no rest for the sole of her foot, and she returned unto Noah into the ark, for the waters were on the face of the whole earth: then he put forth his hand, and took her, and pulled her in unto him into the ark.*
— Genesis 8:9 NASB

*Look at the birds of the air; they do not sow or reap or store away in barns, and yet your heavenly Father feeds them. Are you not much more valuable than they?*
— Matthew 6:26 NIV

## MOMENT OF REFLECTION

_____

_____

_____

_____

_____

_____

_____

_____

_____

_____

# Day 17

## GOOD MEDICINE

Being a caregiver is no joking matter. However, sometimes situations can seem so challenging, that the only response is to laugh . . . silly laughter, nervous laughter, frustrated laughter, and even confused laughter. Perhaps you may have heard the expression, "It hurt so much; all I could do was laugh in order to keep from crying!" Each day, caregivers MUST find something that brings a smile to their face. It is so important to find something to laugh about. Laughter is the best medicine!

Every day we need to take necessary nutrients into our body to be able to sustain our physical health. We also need joy and laughter in order to sustain our mental and emotional health. Watch a comedy series or a silly movie. Read a funny book or one that has jokes and riddles. Allow a child to *explain* their artwork to you. There are so many ways to incorporate laughter into your life. Pray to find something different to laugh about each day. It is not just good for you, but also it is healing for the one you take care of. It will bring you both a renewed mental, emotional and spiritual strength. Be blessed and LAUGH!

*A cheerful heart is good medicine, but a broken spirit*
*saps a person's strength.*

— Proverbs 17:22 NLT

# MOMENT OF REFLECTION

# Day 18

## WELL KEPT

There are so many demands placed on caregivers, that it takes great effort just to be able to keep your mind and heart clear on a daily basis. There is so much "clutter" that can take over our lives. Appointments, dates, times, people, medications and routines – there is so much to keep track of. Unfortunately, in order to keep it altogether, caregivers often sacrifice their own well-being. If the caregiver is not "well-kept" how then shall he or she maintain the care of another? It is important for caregivers to, above all, "guard their heart and mind." These two essential areas are important to one's emotional and mental health. Being a caregiver is an extremely emotional and difficult mental challenge. It can be hard to watch as a loved one struggles daily through life. The inability to change the situation or to "make it all better" pulls at the heart and mind. God knows this. Such vulnerability reminds us that we cannot do this alone. We need to call upon the Lord and tell Him all that concerns us, so that we can obtain peace in the midst of a difficult situation.

*Be anxious for nothing, but in everything by prayer and supplication, with thanksgiving, let your requests be made known to God; and the peace of God, which surpasses all understanding, will guard your hearts and minds through Christ Jesus.*

— Philippians 4:6-7 NKJV

# Moment of Reflection

# Day 19

## WHO'S KEEPING WATCH?

It can be a challenge to "keep watch" all the time. We are human! We get tired. We shut down and easily lose focus when our strength is gone. I remember the first night I brought my mother home with me from the hospital after her stroke. The hospital bed was set up in the family room and the couch was positioned where I could see her. After weeks of running back and forth to the hospital, meeting with doctors, making arrangements with social workers and fighting with insurance companies, I was TIRED! Then I read the discharge slip again, as if I possibly could not have heard the doctor clearly, "Please watch overnight to make sure that patient is breathing well while sleeping." "Are you kidding me? How was I going to be able to do that?" I remember being extremely tired and it was only 8:00 at night! It was a struggle and I can't recall the number of times my head bobbed up and down. I could feel my eyeballs like two weighted marbles I was trying hard to keep in place. I felt so guilty. What if something happened while I was sleeping? I knew that it was important to stay awake. Staying awake all night was literally the "doctor's orders." However, because I was so tired, my mind was numb to the urgency and priority of staying alert. After the first two nights of barely staying awake while my mom looked more restful than she had in weeks, I realized that I did not have the strength needed to make sure that my mom was going to be alright at all times. It was the will of God and the grace of God that would have to keep her. It gave me peace to know that ultimately, God was the one who was keeping watch over my mother. Her life was in His hands.

Matthew 26 and Mark 14 both give an account of the sovereignty of God's will. It is Jesus' last moment before he was betrayed by Judas and destined to die on the cross. He asked his disciples, his friends, to please keep watch all night, while he prayed about his potentially deadly fate. Every few hours, Jesus would find the disciples sleeping. After the third time, Jesus gave them permission to continue in their rest, knowing that the will of the Father would be done regardless of how alert the disciples were. I can only imagine how the disciples felt when they awoke to find him being taken away with the Roman soldiers. "If only we could have stayed awake!" God knew, however. It was His plan and He was keeping watch.

> *Indeed, he who watches over Israel will neither slumber nor sleep.*
>
> — Psalm 121:4 NIV

## MOMENT OF REFLECTION

_____

_____

_____

_____

_____

_____

_____

_____

_____

_____

_____

# Day 20

## TENSION IN THE HOUSEHOLD

Giving of yourself for others who need you more may seem like "the right thing to do." However, it may be difficult for those closest to you to understand. This is especially true when they think they need you more. In John 11, Martha and Mary, whom Jesus loved, had a great need. Their brother Lazarus was sick and dying. They knew that Jesus could heal Him and wanted Him to come to them immediately. Jesus was ministering in another town and even after hearing of their need, he decided to stay two days longer where he was. After that time, he came to Martha and Mary, who felt that He had let them down. "How could you not be here for us when we are supposed to have such a close relationship? Why would you stay to help strangers who you may not ever see again causing those who love you most to wait on the sidelines?" Jesus understood that his priority was to do the will of His Father.

It can be a challenge to balance being a caregiver and meeting the needs of other loved ones who also need your attention. It takes a special sensitivity that can only come from prayer. Pray to have an awareness of what the Lord wants you to do each day. Pray about how to maintain other relational commitments and responsibilities to others in your household, who believe that you are not meeting their needs. Pray that God will give you the ability to be obedient to what He has you to do. Loving many people without having a divided heart is challenging. No one can tell you how to make everyone happy nor can you ever expect to please everyone. Prayer is your greatest tool towards achieving an inward peace in the midst of great tension.

*Now Martha said to Jesus, "Lord, if You had been here, my brother would not have died.*

— John 11:21 NKJV

## MOMENT OF REFLECTION

# *Day 21*

## THE ADVOCATE

"Are you her daughter?", asked the nurse. "Yes, I am," I replied. "Good, wait here while I go get the doctor who wants to speak with you." It was the moment of truth. I was presented with a challenge beyond my emotional or rational ability. As I watched my mother lying in the hospital bed, I knew that she could not speak up for herself. She would not be able to represent her needs or her wants. She needed an advocate. What was I supposed to do? What was I supposed to say? NOTHING in my life's experience had prepared me for that moment. I soon learned that the best way that I could advocate for my mother, was to really watch, listen and study her. I learned to communicate with her, through interpreting her glances and tugs on my fingers. It took time! Each passing week, however, it became easier. The nurses and doctors knew medicine, but they did not know my mom. It was important that she was acknowledged and responded to as a person, not just a patient! I had to learn how to boldly and graciously make those in the medical community understand that she still had a voice; I was her advocate.

*...We have an advocate who pleads our case...*

— I John 2:1 NLT

# Moment of Reflection

# Day 22

## VEGETATED

"Vegetated!" I laughed to myself, when I saw that this word was actually in the dictionary. It is an expression that I often used to describe moments when I was focused on nothing, doing nothing and thinking about nothing. It was anytime I could find to escape to my recliner, put my legs up, sip tea and breathe slowly and deeply. If only for a half hour, being "vegetated" brought me renewal and peace. I often found it hard to peel myself out of the chair and get back up to face my reality. At first, I would feel guilty, knowing there was so much to be done. My mind was always racing to stay on top of my schedule: Get mom dressed, make a meal, spoon feed the meal, administer the medicine, clean up after her, clean up after myself, get ready to do it all over again -- three and sometimes four times a day. I needed those brief moments just to vegetate. After I was done vegetating, I was ready and grateful for the moment I'd had to take care of me.

> *Come to me all who are weary and heavy laden and I will give you rest.*
>
> — Matthew 11:28 NASB

# Moment of Reflection

# Day 23

## SIMPLE PLEASURES

I remember praying to God one day about feeling like I was in a valley of repetition. A few days had passed by. Each day was spent in the same room, following the same routine and watching the same television shows. It was summer, yet the only warmth to be felt was from the blankets I wrapped my mom up in so she would not get so cold from the air conditioner. I needed a change of scenery! I got her dressed, put her into her wheelchair and we rolled outside. I don't know why I had not done that before. I was too focused on thinking that if we went outside, we would have to "go" somewhere. As I rolled the chair to the front of the house and felt the hot sun on my head, I looked down at my mother who was smiling. I took off our shoes, so we could feel the warm grass on our feet. I couldn't have paid for a better vacation spot. The change of scenery we needed was right there in my yard – our valley of love and delight.

There's a beautiful song that says:

> 'Tis the gift to be simple,
> 'tis the gift to be free,
> 'tis the gift to come down
> where we ought to be,
> and when we find ourselves in the place just right,
> 'twill be in the valley of love and delight.

# Moment of Reflection

# Day 24

## ABOVE AND BEYOND

As a caregiver, I was blessed to have two sisters who were very supportive. One sister, though living on the other side of the country, was committed to praying. It was a comfort and a joy to know that every daily circumstance and challenge was lifted in prayer. My other sister, who was closer, yet still an hour away, made every effort to come by and help out several days a week. Sometimes, she even stayed overnight in order to help in the morning. There were those times, however, when an urgent and immediate need would arise. I would have to call on friends and neighbors, who were able to help at a moment's notice. When I think back to those who were willing and who always availed themselves as a support, I often feel quite overwhelmed with gratitude. Women and men from my community and church brought meals, helped clean my house, did laundry, and most significantly, many assisted me in taking care of my four small, young children between one and five years of age. It amazes me when I reflect back to the nights that I laid awake trying to figure out how the next day was going to work out. Inevitably, the following night, I was thanking God for the peaceful close of another day.

*...There's a friend who sticks closer than a brother.*
— Proverbs 18:24 NASB

# Moment of Reflection

# Day 25

## THE CARETAKER GPS

How wonderful it would be if every caregiver had a GPS system that helped them to navigate through each day. There are doctor's orders, social worker recommendations and friendly suggestions given by friends and family who have the best intentions. In reality, it is the caregiver who ultimately has to exercise their judgment in caring for their loved one. Sometimes the goal is just to make it to the end of another day knowing that the one you are caring for is safe and you are still sane.

Family and friends may inquire, "Are you...?, Did you...?, Shouldn't you...? Have you thought about...?" he questions can end up causing more stress and anxiety than necessary. As challenging as it can be, sometimes you just have to tune out the voices of criticism and focus solely on what can be done with the time and resources available at the moment. Caregiving is not an exact science with universal instructions and procedures. Caregiving is a process that takes time. With time, comes experience and the ability to develop a routine. There is no one absolute right or wrong way to care for another. Every situation and relationship is different. There is no magic wand to make a tough situation better. Seek sound advice from the doctor and other professional support, but ultimately be prayerful and realistic about what responsibilities you can fulfill to ensure the well-being of the one you are caring for.

*You guide me with your counsel, leading me to a glorious destiny.*

— Psalm 73:24 NLT

# Moment of Reflection

# Day 26

## THE BEAUTY OF BOUNDARIES

There's an expression that says, "Good fences make good neighbors." This is especially true as a caregiver. It can be hard to establish certain boundaries, when so much of your life is suddenly being shared with another. You also have those well-meaning dear ones who want to be kept updated on how the care is going. It may be challenging to respond to every phone call or to receive each visitor who wants to know what you need. A friend of mine, while taking care of her mother with cancer, said the phone calls and visitors had become so overwhelming that even her mother just wanted to be left alone at times. She came up with an idea to leave her mother's "status" on the voice mail. It was a huge stress reliever. Now, there are even social media sites and healthcare blog sites that caregivers can direct friends and family to so that they can view updates on your loved one's treatments and care. While personal touch and interaction are important to encourage health, time and rest are equally important, which makes alternative communication outlets so necessary. Caregivers must establish periods of rest that are free from overwhelming distractions.

> *[Nehemiah] commanded that the gates of Jerusalem should be shut and not to be opened until the Sabbath [the day of rest] ended.*
>
> — Nehemiah 13:19 NLT

# Moment of Reflection

# Day 27

## THE JOY OF THE LORD

It was a special day for the people of Israel. The Bible tells the account of how the walls of Jerusalem had to be rebuilt and of the great work and labor that it took to complete the project. Upon completion, the governor of Israel, Nehemiah, gathered all the people together. It must have been quite an event. I have been to several ceremonies, where a ribbon placed at the front of an edifice was cut and certain dignitaries were asked to stand as witnesses to the completion of another fine project. What I did not see were the nameless individuals who physically labored for days, weeks and sometimes years to make the vision a reality. Then I think back to Jews in the days of Nehemiah, who must have been overwhelmed as they stood for the ceremonial acknowledgment of the completion of the walls of Jerusalem. It must have been overwhelming to see such a sight, knowing that they had spent countless days and sacrificed their own lives to erect the wall, which was also a symbol of a rebuilding of their faith. This moment culminated with a public reading of the Law of Moses, which reminded the people that they were a nation of God again. They were finally able to rest now. How did they respond? They wept. What a reaction! In fact, Nehemiah had to instruct the people that it was all right to go celebrate after they had been conditioned for so long to labor and sacrifice. I can only imagine the countless lives that were lost in the construction of the building. There were inevitably many other people who were probably sick, bruised or maimed. Now, they are instructed to go forth and with joy? It can be hard to labor every day and then be told to have joy. It almost does not seem right, but that is what God calls us to do. We have to treat each day as sacred to our Lord and not grieve over what was or is, but rather allow the joy of the Lord to be our strength.

> *Go and enjoy choice food and sweet drinks, and send some to those who have nothing prepared. This day is sacred to our Lord. Do not grieve, for the joy of the LORD is your strength.*
>
> — Nehemiah 8:10 NIV

## MOMENT OF REFLECTION

_____

_____

_____

_____

_____

_____

_____

_____

_____

_____

_____

_____

_____

_____

_____

# Day 28

## YOU ARE A GREAT TREASURE

How do you spend your time when you are alone? Caregivers can spend so much time looking after the concerns of others that it becomes easy to neglect personal enjoyment. Perhaps you no longer do the things that you used to enjoy. It may be time to find a new treasure, a hobby that brings value and pleasure to your day. Hobbies have been known to reduce stress and improve the well-being of a person. There are many options and pastimes, but regardless of which one you choose, if it becomes valuable enough to you, it will bring joy to your heart. Some hobbies include writing, reading, crocheting, stamp collecting, art, and music. Your hobby can become your treasure and add value to your life and to the life of the one you care for.

I have learned from a dear friend, Nadia, that it is important to know when you need a break as a caregiver. It may not be easy, but caregivers have to make their well-being a priority, even if it is only for a few hours. Caregivers need to find ways to uplift themselves emotionally, physically, mentally and spiritually. Find ways to let others know that you need a break. Some are able to pay for the services of a caregiving agency. Others may not have the resources to do that. In that case, boldly reach out to a local church, community center, volunteer organization, neighbor or family to see if someone is available to give you the moments to yourself that you desperately need.

*Restore to me the joy of Your salvation, And uphold me by Your generous Spirit.*

— Psalm 51:12 NKJV

# Moment of Reflection

# *Day 29*

## PRIVILEGED TO BE A COMFORTER

I was fortunate to move next door to some amazing neighbors. One day while talking with the wife, she asked me if I had met her husband. I said, of course. She then recounted how they met in college and what an amazing man he was. In fact, he was still her boyfriend. Soon after, I realized that she had Alzheimer's and the disease progressed quickly over a few years to the degree that she started forgetting who I was. Her husband cared for her, as if this change in his wife was not a certain reality. He made sure she was dressed every day, had her hair done and took her frequently to get a manicure. She always looked beautiful and expressed how beautiful he always made her feel. He attended to her every need at every hour of the day and night. I could tell he was tired and hurting to see his beautiful bride struggle with memory loss. I would often visit to sit and talk with her, so that her husband could run errands or teach a class. I know it was a small gesture compared to what he did all day, every day for her, but I could tell that it meant so much to him to be able to take a moment for himself.

When a neighbor falls, do we help them up? When a loved one cannot care for themselves, do we help out? What a privilege it is to be called to be a comforter. There is no greater job or responsibility that a person can fulfill, than to be a comforter to someone who is feeling oppressed by various health challenges. It is often our willingness to *see* others in the midst of their affliction that brings much comfort. Because we are blessed to be "with strength," we are able to be a comfort to others.

*I observed all the oppression that takes place under the sun. I saw the tears of the oppressed, with no one to comfort them. The oppressors have great power, and their victims are helpless... BUT two people are better off than one, for they can help each other succeed. If one person falls, the other can reach out and help. But someone who falls alone is in real trouble.*

— Ecclesiastes 4:1-3, 9-10 NLT

## MOMENT OF REFLECTION

_____

_____

_____

_____

_____

_____

_____

_____

_____

_____

_____

_____

_____

_____

_____

_____

# Day 30

## ON YOUR BEHALF

When my mother came home after being in the hospital for several weeks, she was weak and totally dependent. She could not stand up, get dressed or eat on her own. I was in control. After a few weeks, however, this all began to change. She got stronger and wanted to be less dependent. She even began to make demands about what she wanted, despite the doctor's recommendations. "Leave me in bed! I don't want to wear that! Give me the sugar and salt!" The days were challenging enough before. Now, they were LONG and challenging. Knowing the potential struggles that awaited me made me feel like I wanted to scream before the day even began. One morning, while lying in bed thinking about my day, I began to pray. "Lord, prepare me for this day! What should I do first?" Immediately, these words came to my mind: "Before you get up, get down." I rolled out of bed and got down on the ground and began to praise God for the strength he had given me. It was then that I took each concern to prayer, knowing that there was nothing I could do to persuade my mother. However, I could pray that God would speak to her heart, so that she could humbly receive the things that were being said to her by those who loved and cared for her.

> *Give all your worries and cares to God, for he cares about you.*
>
> — I Peter 5:7 NLT

# Moment of Reflection

# Day 31

## BLESSED ASSURANCE

Sometimes the day to day routine can blind us to the fact that there is an eternal hope which is greater than what we can see in the present moment. The Book of Hebrews is a wonderful reflection of God's fulfillment of the promises He makes to those who put their trust in Him. Like Fanny Crosby, a woman who was made blind by a doctor's mistake when she was only six weeks old, God gave her a story and a song. Each of us, regardless of what we do or who we are, can ask God to give us a story and a song to remind us of the hope that we have been given through faith in Jesus Christ.

*For God is not unjust to forget your work and labor of love which you have shown toward His name, in that you have ministered to the saints, and do ministry. And we desire that each one of you show the same diligence to the full assurance of hope until the end, that you do not become sluggish, but imitate those who through faith and patience inherit the promises.*
*— Hebrews 6:10-12 NKJV*

*Blessed assurance, Jesus is mine!*
*O what a foretaste of glory divine!*
*Heir of salvation, purchase of God,*
*Born of His Spirit, washed in His blood.*

*This is my story, this is my song,*
*Praising my Savior, all the day long;*

*This is my story, this is my song,*
*Praising my Savior, all the day long.*

## MOMENT OF REFLECTION

_____

_____

_____

_____

_____

_____

_____

_____

_____

_____

_____

_____

_____

_____

_____

_____

_____

_____

_____

_____

_____

_____

# Caregiver's Notes

# About the Author

Dr. Chelsea Foster is an educator who has been teaching for 25 years. Most importantly, she is a mother of four caring and creative teens and has a courageous husband, to whom she has been married for over 20 years. Dr. Chelsea has spent over thirty years as a caregiver for immediate and extended family, her four children and for her neighbors, as needed. Her heart for caregivers is that they know that they are not just giving  care, but they are cared about. As caregivers, we need to press forward to find ways to make sure to take care of ourselves with all our heart, mind, soul and body.

For information about speaking engagements, workshops, or consulting, please send an email to drchelseacares@gmail.com.

*Take care!*